German Phrases

A Complete Guide With The Most Useful German Language Phrases While Traveling

Dave Smith

© Copyright 2018 by Dave Smith

All rights reserved.

The following eBook is reproduced below with the goal of providing information that is as accurate and reliable as possible. Regardless, purchasing this eBook can be seen as consent to the fact that both the publisher and the author of this book are in no way experts on the topics discussed within and that any recommendations or suggestions that are made herein are for entertainment purposes only. Professionals should be consulted as needed prior to undertaking any of the action endorsed herein.

This declaration is deemed fair and valid by both the American Bar Association and the Committee of Publishers Association and is legally binding throughout the United States.

Furthermore, the transmission, duplication or reproduction of any of the following work including specific information will be considered an illegal act irrespective of if it is done electronically or in print. This extends to creating a secondary or tertiary copy of the work or a recorded copy and is only allowed with an expressed written consent from the Publisher. All additional rights reserved.

The information in the following pages is broadly considered to be truthful and accurate account of facts, and as such any inattention, use or misuse of the information in question by the reader will render any resulting actions solely under their purview. There are no scenarios in which the publisher or the original author of this work can be in any fashion deemed liable for any hardship or damages that may befall them after undertaking information described herein.

Additionally, the information in the following pages is intended only for informational purposes and should thus be thought of as universal. As befitting its nature, it is presented without assurance regarding its prolonged validity or interim quality. Trademarks that are mentioned are done without written consent and can in no way be considered an endorsement from the trademark holder.

Table of Contents

Introduction 5
Chapter 1: Visiting Germany 7
Chapter 2: A Word About Pronunciation 9
    Short versus Long Vowels 9
Chapter 3: Nouns, Cases and Gender—Oh, my! 12
    Cases 12
    Gender 15
    Articles 16
    Pronouns 17
    Nouns 20
    Adjectives 24
Chapter 4: Verbs 27
    Weak Verbs 28
    Strong verbs 31
    Past Tense 32
    Present Perfect 33
    Past Perfect 35
Chapter 5: Word Order 37
Chapter 6: Fundamental Vocabulary 41
    Days of the Week 41
    Months 41
    Time 42
Chapter 7: Basic Phrases 43
    Getting to Know You... 44
    Small Talk 47
    Shopping 51
    Getting Around 55
    Lodging & Hotels 64
    Eating Out 66
    Emergencies 75
    Holiday Greetings 77
Chapter 8: Putting it All Together 81
Chapter 9: Continuing to Learn 83

Introduction

Ask most people what they would do if money was no object, and almost every time, *travel* will appear in the list. Most of us seem to have a hard-wired desire to visit the places we've read or dreamed about throughout our lives.

Visiting other countries is great for expanding horizons, meeting new people, trying new foods, and promoting cultural understanding. One way of getting the most out of your travel experience is by developing rapport—even to a small extent—with the locals. You will be amazed at how much friendlier and more helpful people are, when you make an attempt to communicate with them in their own language, rather than expecting them to automatically know yours.

English is one of the most widely-studied languages in the world, but that doesn't mean the shopkeepers will be particularly comfortable speaking it. If you're willing to make incompetent and probably amusing attempts to speak German, it will most likely ease their anxiety about attempting to speak English to you. Even though many of them talk to English speakers every day, it's only natural to feel a sense of disadvantage when speaking a language that you're not fluent in. You will find that by making yourself vulnerable first, they will more likely go the extra mile to help you.

While it's unlikely you'll be able to learn the whole language before you go, you can learn some key phrases that you should be able to utilize to impress your traveling companions as well as the people you meet—who will hopefully become friends. As well as the basic phrases, this book also offers some basic grammar to help you understand how the phrases are put together. It will teach you pronouns, basic verb conjugation, case, gender, tense, and the fundamentals of sentence structure, such as when word order is reversed, when verbs are moved to the end, etc. Once you have a feel for the basics, you can begin adding the vocabulary. Once you have some vocabulary, it will be easier for you to start recognizing words and phrases in the conversations going on around you; at that point, your ability to learn the language will begin to grow exponentially.

Each phrase is accompanied by a pronunciation guide that should help you wrap your tongue around the words. Keep in mind that very few sounds translate exactly from one language to another. You will not, at first, be able to pronounce German words like a native speaker would, and of course, this will be awkward for you and probably amusing for your hosts and new friends. This is only natural and something every language learner goes through. But if you listen carefully to native speakers and ask for their help, you can develop the ability to approximate the sounds of German to a large degree.

Chapter 1: Visiting Germany (and Other German-Speaking Countries)

Germany, Austria and Switzerland are beautiful places and lots of fun to visit. No matter what time of year you go, there are many fascinating possibilities for entertainment and sightseeing. Check out the many resources on the web for lists of the many places you'll want to visit. And your trip will be greatly enhanced if you can make some friends while you're there.

Whether you're heading to Germany for a gorgeous river cruise on the Rhine, planning on a rousing Oktoberfest party, skiing in the Alps or attending the Frankfurt Book Fair, you can enhance your trip drastically if you find ways to immerse yourself in the culture, including the language.

It isn't necessary to become fluent in German before packing your bags. As a matter of fact, every German student studies English, and even if they aren't comfortable practicing it in front of a native speaker, many of them will be able to communicate with you on some level, especially if you show them that you're willing to make an effort.

Even if you're not fluent (or particularly conversant), it goes a long way if you make an attempt to talk to people in their own language. At the very least, they will feel less ridiculous speaking in halting English if you're reciprocating, by putting your new ability in German on display. Being able to laugh at your own mistakes will make them feel better about theirs, and they are more likely to go the extra step to try to help you. It also shows respect for their culture and demonstrates your willingness to make an effort to connect with them. If you can use some basic German, there is less of a chance of being cheated by deceitful tourist traps!

While it's not possible to learn any language in a few days, it will certainly speed up your efforts if you understand some of the basics of the German language, especially in the ways it differs from English. You can learn phrases and practice them with the people you meet, but without understanding the mechanics of the language, you won't retain them well or be able to use them to make other sentences and grow your language skills. This book will teach you the basic things you need to know to begin building sentences. You will learn noun cases, pronouns, articles and adjectives, verb conjugation, and tenses. Once you have a basic knowledge of the language, you can begin to plug in vocabulary and fine tune your sentence-building skills.

If you happen to be spending time in a country where you can immerse yourself in German, you can become conversant to at least a moderate degree in a surprisingly short time. Listen as much as you can, ask questions about things that you don't understand, and read everything—from billboards to receipts. It's amazing how fast you will begin to recognize words, phrases, grammar points and sentence structure. And you will find that the natives, once they know you are determined to learn, will take a great amount of pleasure in coaching you!
Following is a short primer on German pronunciation and the fundamentals of German grammar, so that you can begin to get a feel for how the language works.

Chapter 2: A Word About Pronunciation

For the most part, there are only a few rules you will need to learn to be able to work out the pronunciation of German words to a moderately acceptable level.

Short versus Long Vowels

In English we have the concept of "short" and "long" vowels, but that description has very little to do with the way the letter is actually pronounced. Have you ever wondered why the "E" in "bed" is called "short," while the e in "heel" is called "long"? Those words have very little to do with describing the sounds of the vowels.

Not so in most other languages. While the rules for when a vowel is long or short are similar (mostly to do with following other vowels), the pronunciation is much more logical than in English. Short "A" for example, is pronounced "ah." Long "A" is pronounced "aah." Simple, right?

It is actually quite intuitive, once you understand the basics. Of course there are exceptions. In German, the same as in English, there are words that have been borrowed from other languages, so the pronunciation does not necessarily match the spelling conventions of the language. That is unfortunately unavoidable, and something you will have to deal with no matter which language you study. Take heart, though, knowing that English is probably the hardest language to learn in that respect, and you've already mastered that one!

Here are the basic sounds of the German language:

Vowel sounds
a – pronounced "ah" in almost every instance
ä – pronounced ĕ, or "eh"
e – pronounced "ay" when long, ĕ or ə when short. An e at the end of a word is almost always voiced, usually by ə, a simple, unstressed short ĕ sound.
i – pronounced ĭ, like "pit," when short, "ee" when long
o – pronounced "oh"
ö – there is not an English equivalent; it's closest to the "I" in "girl" but you make your lips more rounded
u – pronounced "oo"
ű – "oo" but more exaggerated. To approximate it, say "ee" and then push your lips forward.
y – not usually a vowel, except in certain foreign words. In those words (like "typisch") it's pronounced like "oo" but with very rounded lips.

Diphthongs
(two letters combined to make a "single" sound)
au – pronounced "ow"
äu – pronounced "oy"
eu – also pronounced "oy"
ei – pronounced like "eye"
ie – pronounced "ee"

Consonants
(Most are the same as in English, with the following exceptions)
b – At the closing off of a word or in front of a silent consonant it is voiceless (like the English "P").
c – "C" is very rarely found by itself in German, and most of the time it is, or is found at the beginning of a word, it has been

imported from another language. While in those words it's generally pronounced as it is in the foreign words, in certain cases it's pronounced like the beginning sound of "tsar," in others like "chain." There isn't an actual rule here. You just have to know the words.

d – At the closing off of a word or in front of a silent consonant it is voiceless (like the English "T").

g – It's hard, like "gold," except at the closing off of a word or in front of a silent consonant, when it is voiceless (like the English "K").

qu – Pronounced "kv"

s – At the beginning of a word it's pronounced "v" unless it's paired with a voiceless consonant. Whenever it's with a voiceless consonant it is pronounced "sh."

v – Always voiceless, like the English "F"

w – Pronounced "v"

z – Pronounced "ts"

β – This substitutes for "ss" after a long vowel or a diphthong (except in Switzerland, where they write out the "ss"). It doesn't affect the pronunciation; it's just a writing convention.

ch – This is an odd one. It is roughly pronounced "sh," but when you say it, bring your tongue slightly upward and forward and pull your lips back a bit, keeping them slightly rounded. It sounds a bit like a cat hissing, but the "s" is softer. It takes a bit of practice to get this sound right, but don't worry too much about it—it's pronounced differently in different parts of the German-speaking world, and differently again in other Germanic languages like Dutch, where it is considerably harder. For pronunciation, we will use "kh" to signify this sound.

Chapter 3: Nouns, Cases and Gender—Oh, my!

Cases

This is a good time to discuss this case. In English we aren't used to talking about noun cases, because our cases are simplified to the point they are just taught as a variation of the word without much explanation. For example, as a child you are taught to say "I saw him" instead of "I saw he" or "me saw him." This is simply *the way it is*. We don't usually bother to clarify that "I" and "me" are different cases, although we do learn (and generally forget soon afterwards) that the closest word to being the direct object of the sentence is "me", and so it differs from its subject. It doesn't occur to most of us to wonder why pronouns change when they act as direct objects but other nouns do not. We're also taught that possessives require special treatment, and that also becomes just *the way it is*. But when we learn possessives like "my car" or "my son's bike" we are also using case, although we tend not to think of it that way.

German has a much more complicated case system than English does, and most students find this very intimidating. Rightly so, because it is a foreign concept to most of us and requires some work to conquer, but take heart. It is certainly possible to make yourself understood even when your mastery of case endings is not perfect. And it will come easier with time, practice and a little determination.

German has four cases. For simplicity, we'll call the first one the subjective case because it's usually the subject of the sentence. If you go on to study the language in other venues, you will probably see it referred to as the nominative case, but it's easier to remember when you relate "subject" to "subjective." This is the case of the pronoun forms "I," "he/she," "we," or "they." Remember that we're talking mostly about pronouns because that is where case usually shows up in English. Most nouns are no different in the position of subject than direct object: "The cat is on the bed" versus "Have you seen the cat?"

The next case is the objective case, because it's usually the direct object. Again, you will also see that this is called the accusative case, but we will stick with the more descriptive title. This is the case you're using when you say "me," "him/her," "them," or "us." (Many people have confusions with "who" and "whom" because of the traditional insistence that the objective case of "who" to be used, even though it is a dying distinction in English.)

The third case is called the dative, and we don't really use it in English. This is generally used with (or in place of) prepositions. (Think of it as "going ON a date," and it may help.)

Prepositions in German are confusing at best. Of course when you use a preposition it is followed by a noun ("under the table," "around the corner," "through the door"). These nouns in German need to take either the objective or the dative case, depending on the preposition they're being used with, and the only way to remember which is which—is to memorize them. Unfortunately, there's no other logic to it than that.

Here is a list of common prepositions that take the objective case:

without	**ohne**	ō'-nə
against, toward	**gegen**	gā'-gen
along	**entlang**	ĕnt-lŏng
until	**bis**	bĭs
around	**um**	um
for	**für**	fyur
through, across	**durch**	doorsh

Here is a list of common prepositions that take the dative case:

from	**aus**	ous
except for	**ausser**	ous'-er
by, at	**bei**	bī
of, from	**von**	fŏn
for, since	**seit**	zīt
after	**nach**	nokh
with	**mit**	mĭt
to	**zu**	tzoo
opposite	**gegenüber**	gā-gen-oo-ber
under	**unter**	un'-ter

The fourth case is the easiest to remember: the possessive case. We just think of it as expressing possession, but it is an actual case, even in English, marked by the apostrophe plus s, or the use of "my," "your," "his/her," "their," and "our." If you're wondering how a noun would be possessive without a possessive pronoun, think of it as "of the ____." So, just as in English "the man's wife" could also be expressed as "the wife of the man," in German you could say "der Manns Frau" or "die Frau des Mannes."

Gender

There is one more complicating factor that affects the cases. That is the presence of male, female and "neuter" nouns. This may seem like an obvious and unimportant detail, but keep in mind that all articles, pronouns and adjectives must match the noun's gender and case. In English we only think of gender when it is obvious, and we only mark it for people. While the gender of many nouns is what you'd expect, that is not always the case, and you definitely can't count on it. In German it is perfectly acceptable to speak of a girl as "it" since the German word for girl (das Mädchen) is neuter, but generally you would only do that if you've just used the word Mädchen. Don't stress out too much about that, though. It's also perfectly acceptable (and will probably keep you safer from embarrassment, not to mention brain damage!) to use "she" if you're talking about an actual girl, "he" if you're talking about a masculine cat, and "she" if you're referring to a female dog.

The subjective case is not too difficult to deal with in terms of noun gender. Granted, you will find yourself confused and wracking your brain trying to remember if you've heard "der," "das" or "die" used with the word before, but at least there are only three choices there. Although, when it comes to the other cases, the prospect becomes much more daunting. Learning how to select the dative and possessive versions of an article or pronoun is the bane of many German language learners' existence and much too complicated to expect yourself to conquer in a lesson or two.

The best thing you can do to help yourself with this, is to keep in mind that when you learn a German verb, memorize the article with it so that they are linked in your mind. If you repeat "der Hund" (the dog) rather than simply "Hund," it's much more likely to come to mind later when you need it. Then it'll simply be a matter of figuring out which case you're using and what the ending will be. The most effective technique is to get a good handle on the article and pronoun endings, take a guess at the gender if it isn't obvious, and hope for the best. Don't spend a lot of time doing mental gymnastics trying to fit all of the right endings to your articles, adjectives, and nouns—or else you'll never get through a conversation! Fortunately, most Germans are too polite (and will be too impressed with your valiant efforts) to give you much grief if your endings aren't exactly right. They may smile, and they will almost undoubtedly correct you (they *are* German, after all) but it's almost always in a playful or helpful way. They understand the complexities of their language and for the most part, they'll be sympathetic.

Articles

The main thing you need to know backwards and forwards is articles. While the table looks daunting, it's not too difficult to memorize, and later you'll be using it so much, that it will soon be second nature. It's well worth taking a little time to get a good handle on the case differences and their articles. Once you are familiar with that, it will be much easier to translate it to pronouns and then to adjectives.

Article	Nominative	Objective	Dative	Possessive
the (male)	der	den	dem	des
the (neuter)	das	das	dem	des
the (female)	die	der	der	die
the (plural)	die	die	den	der
a (male)	ein	einen	einem	eines
a (neuter)	ein	ein	einem	eines
a (female)	eine	eine	einer	einer
a (plural)	eine	eine	einen	einer

Notice that the endings of ein-words (indirect articles) are mostly identical to direct article (der/die/das) endings. This is true for every case, except masculine, neuter subjective, and neuter objective. In those cases, there is no ending. This is worth noting, since it will come up again.

Other words that you might see in place of articles are "dies" ("this" or "that") or "welche" (which, what, that, who). The words Der, Die, and Das all share their endings.
Articles are often occasionally used as pronouns (as in "The man that sat in front of me..."). In this case "the" and "that" would both be the subjective definite article ("der"). It's just something worth noting for later.

Pronouns

So, let's move on to German pronouns. The main pronoun cases are shown in the table below. Remember that objective and dative both correspond to the English "me," "him/her," "them," and "us." (Obviously, in English "you" does not change, singular or plural, except in the possessive. Unfortunately, this is not the case in German.) Possessives take the same suffixes as the articles above. If this is a foreign concept to you, take off the "ein" from the indefinite article ("a"). What remains is what will need to be added to the pronoun.

Pronoun	Subjective	Objective	Dative	Possessive
I	ich	mich	mir	mein
you (informal)	du	dich	dir	dein
you (formal)	Sie (always capitalized)	Sie	Ihnen	Ihr
he	er	ihn	ihm	sein
she	sie	sie	ihr	ihr
it	es	es	ihm	sein
we	wir	uns	uns	unser
you (plural)	ihr	euch	euch	euer
they	sie	sie	ihnen	ihrer

Note that there are two forms of singular "you." "Sie" is the formal or polite version. It is used when addressing someone that you would not call by their first name, such as a new acquaintance, an older person, or an authority figure. With family, friends, and children, use the informal "du." When in doubt, follow the lead of the person you are talking to, or listen to how others address each other.

The next things to know are the endings for the possessive case. If this seems confusing, remember that possessives are paired with nouns, and nouns require gender markers. In the same way that you need to determine whether a noun takes "der," "die" or "das," you need to know what to put on the end of your possessive pronoun to agree with the noun.

Possessive Pronouns
Masculine

Masculine noun case:	Subjective	Objective	Dative	Possessive
my	mein	meinen	meinem	meines
your (informal)	dein	deinen	deinem	deines
your (formal)	Sein	Seinen	Seinem	Seines
his	ihr	ihren	ihrem	ihres
her	sein	seinen	seinem	seines
our	unser	unseren	unserem	unseres
your (plural)	euer	euren	eurem	eures
their	ihr	ihren	ihrem	ihres

Feminine

Feminine noun case:	Subjective	Objective	Dative	Possessive
my	meine	meine	meiner	meiner
your (informal)	deine	deine	deiner	deiner
your (formal)	Seine	Seine	Seiner	Seiner
his	ihre	ihre	ihrer	ihrer
her	seine	seine	seiner	seiner
our	unsere	unsere	unserer	unserer
your (plural)	eure	eure	eurer	eurer
their	ihr	ihre	ihrer	ihrer

Neuter

Neuter noun case:	Subjective	Objective	Dative	Possessive
my	mein	mein	meinem	meines
your (informal)	dein	dein	deinem	deines
your (formal)	Sein	Sein	Seinem	Seines
his	ihr	ihr	ihrem	ihres
her	sein	sein	seinem	seines
our	unser	unser	unserem	unseres
your (plural)	euer	euer	eurem	eures
their	ihr	ihr	ihrem	Ihres

Plural

Plural noun case:	Subjective	Objective	Dative	Possessive
my	meine	meine	meinen	meiner
your (informal)	deine	deine	deinen	deiner
your (formal)	Seine	Seine	Seinen	Seiner
his	ihre	ihre	ihren	ihrer
her	seine	seine	seinen	seiner
our	unsere	unsere	unseren	unserer
your (plural)	eure	eure	euren	eurer
their	ihr	ihre	ihren	ihrer

If all of those endings look intimidating, note that they are the same as the endings for the indefinite article "ein." Once you have those memorized, it is easy to apply them to your possessive pronouns.

An important note: there are a few relative pronouns in German that are very handy to know. They are **dessen, deren** and **denen**. They all mean "*whose,*" as in:

> "That's the boy *whose* mother works in my office."

Dessen is used for male and neuter nouns and **deren** is used for feminine and plural nouns. In this example you would use **dessen**, referring to "boy," rather than **deren** for "mother." **Denen** is used with plurals in the dative case. Remember that the dative case is used with many prepositions, such as "with."

> "Those are the boys *with* whom my son plays."

You would use **denen** for this, since "boys" is plural and the "with" calls for a dative pronoun.

Nouns

Nouns in German, as you may or may not know, are always capitalized. This can be helpful to a beginning student because you can see immediately which words in the sentence are nouns, taking out some of the analysis. This is a very simple rule, and once you get used to it, it shouldn't cause you any headaches.

Plurals in German are formed in several possible ways:
- adding an "e" (**"der Hund, die Hunde"**) (the dog)
- adding an "n" (**"die Woche, die Wochen"**) (the week)
- adding "er" (**"das Kind, die Kinder"**) (the child)
- putting an umlaut on the vowel (**"der Baum, die Bäume"**) (the tree)
- changing the vowel and adding a suffix (**"der Zug, die Züge"**) (the train)

German nouns also take an "s" in the possessive case, although they do not use an apostrophe as we do in English. There are a few other instances of nouns changing to match their case, but as a beginning student, it's understandable if you don't have them memorized. That can come later.

There is no substitute for good old memorization when it comes to learning noun genders, but there are a few tips that will help. (Of course, you have to memorize these too, but it will make things easier later!)

Der – When you see words that have the following suffixes, chances are they are masculine:
- -ich
- -us
- -ant
- -ast
- -ismus
- -us
- -ling

Die – When you see words that have the following suffixes, chances are they are feminine:
- -enz/-anz
- -ie
- -ur
- -in
- -keit/-heit
- -schaft
- -tät
- -tion/-sion
- -ung
- -ei
- -in
- -ur

Das – When you see words that have the following suffixes, chances are they are neuter:
- -chen
- -lein
- -um

Common Nouns

afternoon	der Nachmittag	nokh'-mit-tak
baby	das Baby	bā'-bē
bed	das Bett	bet
boy	der Junge	yoong-ə
breakfast	das Frühstück	froo'-shtook
brother	der Bruder	broo'-der
building	das Gebäude	ge-boy'-də
business	das Geschäft	ge-sheft'
car	das Auto	ou'-tō
castle	das Schloss	shlos
cell phone	das Handy	hand-ē
chair	der Stuhl	shtool
child	das Kind	kĭnt
city	die Stadt	shtat
coffee	der Kaffee	kah'-fē
corner	die Ecke	eck-ə
daughter	die Tochter	tokh'-ter
day	der Tag	tak
dinner	das Abendessen	ah'-bend-es-en
doctor	der Doktor	doc-tor
dog	der Hund	hoont
door	die Tür	toor
ear	das Ohr	ōr
eye	das Auge	ou-gə
family	die Familie	fa-mē'-lē
father	der Vater	fa'-ter
food	das Essen	ess-en
friend	der Freund (m),	froind, froin'-din

		die Freundin (f)	
girl	das Mädchen		mād'-shən
hair	das Haar		hahr
hand	die Hand		hont
head	der Kopf		kōpf
hotel	das Hotel		hō-tel
hour	die Stunde		shtun-də
house	das Haus		hous
job	der Beruf		be-roof'
lady	die Dame		do'-mə
leg	das Bein		bīn
love	die Liebe		lē'-bə
lunch	das Mittagessen		mĭt-tok'-es-en
man	der Mann		mon
map	die Karte		kar'-tə
minute	die Minute		mĭn-oot'
money	das Geld		gelt
month	der Monat		mō-not
morning	der Morgen		mor'-gen
mother	die Mutter		moot'-er
night	die Nacht		nokht
people	das Volk		folk
person	die Person		pair-zōn'
phone	das Telefon		tele-fōn'
present	das Geschenk		ge-shenk'
problem	das Problem		prō-blām'
question	die Frage		frah'-gə
restaurant	das Restaurant		res-tōr-ont
road/street	die Straße		shtrah'-sə
room	das Zimmer		tzĭm-mer
second	der Zweite		tzvīt
sister	die Schwester		shves'-ter
sky	der Himmel		hĭm-mel
son	der Sohn		zōn
suitcase	der Koffer		kof'-ər
sun	die Sonne		zō'-nə
table	der Tisch		tish
ticket	die Fahrkarte		făr'-kar-tə
time	die Zeit		tzīt

town	die Stadt	*shtat*
toy	Spielzeug	*shpēl'-tzoig*
tree	der Baum	*boum*
view	Aussicht	*ous'-zikht*
water	das Wasser	*vas'-ser*
way	der Weg	*vek*
week	die Woche	*vō'-khə*
window	das Fenster	*fen'-ster*
woman	die Frau	*frou*
year	das Jahr	*yahr*

Adjectives

In German as in English, adjectives come before the noun. Since this is the case, as you might expect—but is dreaded to hear, they need to have endings to match the gender and case.

The bad news here is that you need to take one extra thing into consideration before attaching the ending.

The good news is that it's a bit simpler than it sounds. The adjective does not necessarily have to have something tacked on to it.

Where the noun has a "strong" ending ("einem," "dieses," etc.), the adjective does not need a case ending. Only one of the words preceding the noun needs to carry a "strong" ending. So you would say, for example, "Der schwer Koffer" (the heavy suitcase). Here "schwer" does not take an "er" ending, because it's already present in "der." However, you would have to say "Ein schwerer Koffer," since "ein" does not take an ending in the masculine subjective case. That leaves it to the adjective to carry the strong ending and show gender.

Common Adjectives

whole	**ganz**	*gonts*
large, tall	**groß**	*grōs*
good	**gut**	*goot*
new	**neu**	*neu*
first	**erst**	*erst*
long	**lang**	*long*
German	**deutsch**	*doitsh*
small	**klein**	*klīn*
old	**alt**	*ahlt*
high	**hoch**	*hōkh*
simple	**einfach**	*īn'-fokh*
last	**letzte**	*letzt*
same, right away	**gleich**	*glīkh*
possible	**möglich**	*mōg'-likh*
own	**eigen**	*ī'-gen*
beautiful	**schön**	*shōn*
late	**spat**	*shpāt*
important	**wichtig**	*vikh'-tik*
young	**jung**	*yung*

Practice

Let's try putting some of these concepts together. Translate these noun phrases, making sure you take into consideration the gender and number (singular or plural) of the noun as you assign the appropriate article or pronoun to it.

my dog (nominative)
my beautiful baby (objective)
his ear (dative)
this late hour (nominative)
our money (possessive)

the first morning (dative)
a city (nominative)
your telephone (informal, objective)
my leg (dative)
our house (possessive)
this afternoon (nominative)
their brother (objective)
the old building (possessive)
her son (dative)
your car (formal, objective)
the child whose dog (subjective)

Chapter 4: Verbs

German verbs are much more regular than English verbs. This is very good news for the German student (finally, something simple!). We are used to tenses, and fortunately there are many similarities in that area too.

I am	**ich bin**	*ikh bin*
you are (informal)	**du bist**	*doo bist*
you are (formal singular and plural)	**Sie sind**	*zē sint*
he/she/it is	**er/sie/es ist**	*air/zē/ess ist*
we are	**wir sind**	*veer zint*
you are (plural informal)	**ihr seid**	*eer zīt*
they are	**sie sind**	*zē sint*

Of course, as in English, the fundamental verb "to be" is not quite regular, so let's start there.

I have	**ich habe**	*ikh hŏb-ə*
you have (informal)	**du hast**	*doo host*
you have (formal singular and plural)	**Sie haben**	*zē hŏ'-ben*
he/she/it has	**er/sie/es hat**	*air/zē/ess hŏt*
we have	**wir haben**	*veer hŏ'-ben*
you have (plural informal)	**ihr habt**	*eer hŏbt*
they have	**sie haben**	*zē hŏ'-ben*

The next most important verb, as in English, is "to have." This is used as an auxiliary (or "helping") verb, much as it is in English, with a few exceptions.

Weak Verbs

This conjugation is very close to "regular" or "weak" verbs.

I come	**ich komme**	*ikh kōm-ə*
you come (informal)	**du kommst**	*doo kōmst*
you come (formal singular and plural)	**Sie kommen**	*zē kōm-ən*
he/she/it comes	**er/sie/es kommt**	*air/zē/ess kōmt*
we come	**wir kommen**	*veer kōm-ən*
you come (plural informal)	**ihr kommt**	*eer kōmt*
they come	**sie kommen**	*zē kōm-ən*

Kommen ("to come") is a good example of a weak verb.

As you can see, regular conjugation is fairly simple. Most German verbs follow this same pattern:
I: -**e**
you (informal): -**st**
you (formal, singular and plural): -**en**
he/she/it: -**t**
we: -**en**
you (plural, informal): -**t**
they: -**en**

Another regular but important verb is "to go," **gehen**. Here is its conjugation:

I go	**ich gehe**	*ikh gā'-ə*
you go (informal)	**du gehst**	*doo gāst*
you go (formal singular and plural)	**Sie gehen**	*zē gā'-ən*
he/she/it goes	**er/sie/es geht**	*air/zē/ess gāt*
we go	**wir gehen**	*veer gā'-ən*
you go (plural informal)	**ihr geht**	*eer gāt*
they go	**sie gehen**	*zē gā'-ən*

Note: "To go" is used a bit differently in German. In English we might say, "I am going to Frankfurt" but in German you would say "I am traveling (fahren) to Frankfurt."

Here is a breakdown of the traveling verbs that can be confusing:

- **gehen**: go, move, leave, walk, go down, quit
- **fahren**: run, ride, drive, pass, move
- **kommen**: get, reach, come, arrive, go

These verbs have another unique trait, which will be described in the section on past tense. For now, just keep them in mind as a related group.

Then there is **haben** (to have), an extremely important verb.

I have	**ich habe**	*ikh hăb'-ə*
you have (informal)	**du hast**	*doo hăbt*
you have (formal singular and plural)	**Sie haben**	*zē hăb'-ən*
he/she/it has	**er/sie/es hat**	*air/zē/ess hăt*
we have	**wir haben**	*veer hăb'-ən*
you have (plural informal)	**ihr habt**	*eer hăbt*
they have	**sie haben**	*zē hăb'-ən*

Here is a list of common German regular verbs:

to eat	**essen**	*ess-ən*
to go, drive	**fahren**	*fahr'-ən*
to see	**sehen**	*zā-ən*
to want	**wollen**	*vōl'-ən*
to bring	**bringen**	*bring'-ən*
to think	**denken**	*denk'-ən*
to write	**schreiben**	*shrīb'-ən*
to buy	**kaufen**	*kouf'-ən*
to help	**helfen**	*helf'-ən*
to make	**machen**	*mokh'-en*
to drink	**trinken**	*trink'-ən*
to become	**werden**	*vair'-dən*

Strong verbs

Usually, the main difference between strong and weak verbs is that the vowel changes during conjugation in the second and third person singular. There isn't a hard and fast rule about which verbs are strong, and what their vowels will change into, but it's a pretty decent bet that any newly formed verbs (like "surfen") will be weak.

So a word like "**brechen**" (to break) will conjugate in the following way:

Ich breche, du brichst, Sie brechen, er/sie/es bricht, wir brechen, ihr brecht, sie brechen

may, to be allowed	**dürfen**	darf
to eat	**essen**	ißt
to give	**geben**	gibt
to help	**helfen**	hilft
can, to be able to	**können**	kann
to run	**laufen**	läuft
must	**müssen**	muss
to take	**nehmen**	nimmt
to sleep	**schlafen**	schläft
to speak	**sprechen**	spricht
to meet	**treffen**	trifft

There are too many strong verbs to try to memorize, but there are some that it is imperative to know:

One of the biggest differences between English and German when it comes to verbs is the present tense. In English there is a difference between "I am going" and "I go." In German, the present tense ("I go") serves as the simple or progressive present ("I am going"), the habitual present ("I go every Saturday"), and also the future ("I will go" or "I am going to go").

Past Tense

Simple past is most often formed by adding a **-t** at the end of the word, but often the vowel is changed as well. Many of the strong forms were brought over into English so will already be familiar.

Past tense weak verbs are conjugated in the following way:

I said	**ich sagte**	*ikh zăg'-tə*
you said (informal)	**du sagtest**	*doo zăg'-test*
you said (formal singular and plural)	**Sie sagten**	*zē zăg'-tən*
he/she/it said	**er/sie/es sagt**	*air/zē/ess zăgt*
we said	**wir sagten**	*veer zăgt'-ən*
you said (plural informal)	**ihr sagtet**	*eer zăg'-tet*
they said	**sie sagten**	*zē zăg'-ten*

Past tense strong verbs, as you might expect, can be conjugated in several different ways, but for the most part the endings will be pretty close to weak verb endings.

Here are a few examples:

I went	**ich ging**	*ikh gĭng*
you went (informal)	**du gingst**	*doo gĭngst*
you went (formal singular plural)	**Sie gingen**	*zē gĭng'-ən*
he/she/it went	**er/sie/es ging**	*air/zē/ess gĭng*
we went	**wir gingen**	*veer gĭng'-ən*
you went (plural informal)	**ihr gingt**	*eer gĭngt*
they went	**sie gingen**	*zē gĭng'-en*

I spoke	**ich sprach**	*ikh shprakh*
you spoke (informal)	**du sprachst**	*doo shprakhst*
you spoke (formal singular and plural)	**Sie sprachen**	*zē shprakh'-ən*
he/she/it spoke	**er/sie/es sprach**	*air/zē/ess shprakh*
we spoke	**wir sprachen**	*veer shprakh'-ən*
you spoke (plural informal)	**ihr spracht**	*eer shprakht*
they spoke	**sie sprachen**	*zē shprakh'-en*

Present Perfect

In German, as in English, "to have" is used to make the present perfect in most cases ("I have seen"). One important difference is that some German verbs take "to be" as the auxiliary verb for the perfect tenses. "To be" itself, as well as almost all verbs that mean travelling from one place to another, use this form. So you would say "I am been," "they are gone" or "he is driven" instead of "I have been," "they have gone" or "he has driven." This seems odd to English speakers but really does not take long to get used to.

The past participles (used with the auxiliary verbs "have" or "be") are formed in a few different ways. Most add **ge-** to the beginning of the word, some remove the **-n** or **-en** from the end and add **-t**, and some change their vowels or the form of the middle part.

English	German infinitive	Present	Simple past	Past participle
to go	**gehen**	**geht**	**gang**	**ist gegehen**
to buy	**kaufen**	**kauft**	**kauft**	**hat gekauft**
to help	**helfen**	**hilft**	**half**	**hat geholfen**
to bring	**bringen**	**bringe**	**bracht**	**hat gebracht**
to know (as in facts)	**wissen**	**weißt**	**wußt**	**hat gewußt**
to eat	**essen**	**ißt**	**aß**	**hat gegessen**
to drive/go	**fahren**	**fährt**	**fuhr**	**ist gefahren**
to stay	**bleiben**	**bleibt**	**blieb**	**ist geblieben**
to sleep	**schlafen**	**schläft**	**schlief**	**hat geschlafen**
to lose	**verlieren**	**verliert**	**verlor**	**hat verloren**
to drink	**trinken**	**trinkt**	**trank**	**hat getrunken**
to see	**siehen**	**sieht**	**sah**	**hat gesehen**
to speak	**sprechen**	**spricht**	**sprach**	**hat gesprochen**

There is a group of weak (regular) verbs that take the -**t** at the end but not the beginning **ge**-. These are mostly words that end in -**ieren** like **diskutieren** ("discuss").

Past Perfect

As intimidating as this sound, it's going to be the easiest part of the verb discussion. As a refresher from your school days, past perfect is simply a variation on present perfect tense.

Present Perfect: "I *have* seen that movie" (as of this present moment I have seen the movie)
Past Perfect: "I *had* seen that movie" (at some point in the past when the topic came up, I had already seen the movie)

You create the past perfect simply by using the conjugated past tense of "have," exactly as in English.

There are other, more complicated verb tenses, but there's no need to worry about them at this stage of your learning. They are present in English, too, but as with most aspects of language learning, once you learned to use them as a child, you stopped thinking about how to do it. It is only when you try to transfer the concepts to other languages that you have to re-learn the concepts.

Practice
So let's try some conjugating. Remember there are a couple of things to take into consideration, such as changing vowels, past forms, and modal verbs. Take your time and really start to get a feel for how the language works!
we are eating
you (plural, informal) go
I see
she has spoken
they drive
you (formal) see
I have eaten

we had brought
they have gone
it stayed
you (informal) lost
she will buy
they were drinking
we said

Chapter 5: Word Order

Word order differs between German and English in a few ways that may seem quite confusing at first. However, it is fairly logical and not too difficult to master with just a bit of practice.

Sentence Structure
Simple sentences take the same order as English sentences:
"*I see you,*" "*He wants that.*"

The basic order of a sentence is the subject first, the verb second, followed by the indirect object, and finally the direct object.

"*I am giving a treat to the dog.*" (not "I am giving the dog a treat.")

Normal order of a temporal sentence with location is: Time, manner, place

"*Tomorrow we will go by bus to the mountains.*"

Sentences with two parts connected by the conjunctions "and," "or," "but," and "rather" keep the same order as a simple sentence.

"*She got a cat, but I prefer dogs.*"

Auxiliary Verbs (*must, can, should*, etc.)
This is where it begins to sounds strange to English speakers, but it is actually quite easy to get used to. If you use an

auxiliary verb (sometimes called a "helping verb"), the second verb in the sentence will take the infinitive form (almost always ending in "-en") and comes at the end.

"Can you the book on my desk leave?"

This is also true for the perfect (and past perfect) tense.
"I have nobody seen."

Clauses
<u>Relative clauses</u> (as a refresher, a relative clause can be removed from a sentence without changing its meaning)

In most cases, the verb in a relative clause comes at the end.

"My brother, who in Denver lives, is coming for Christmas."

<u>Subordinate Clauses</u>
"Because I home stayed, missed I the movie."

"Because I stayed home" is a subordinate clause: it cannot stand as a sentence on its own. It is not a relative clause because removing it would change the meaning of the sentence. It would simply be "I missed the movie," without giving the reason.

In German, subordinate clauses are formed by putting the conjunction ("because") first and the verb last. This is a common formation, but when "because," along with a few other select conjunctions (when, if, since, until, that, before, despite, as far as, as soon as, how, while, so that, during, where, as long as) is present, **always** move the verb to the end of a clause.

Notice that when the verb comes at the end of a clause followed by a comma, the next verb is placed immediately following it. This is also known as the "verb comma verb" rule.

"After she dinner ate, did she the dishes."

If the conjunction is in the second clause, the conjugated verb is still moved to the end, but obviously the comma is followed by the conjunction rather than by a verb.

"I will go to work, as long as I better feel."

Verb Inversion

Temporal words at the beginning of a statement cause the verb to be inverted.

"Tomorrow go we to the zoo."

Questions cause the verb to be inverted. Unlike English, auxiliary verbs are not used to create questions.

"Watch you the movie with us?"

Verbs after question words (why, what, who, when, etc.) are inverted, rather than using auxiliary verbs.

"Why said she that?"

Question Words
- Who - **Wer**
- What – **Was**
- Where – **Wo**
- Why – **Warum**
- When – **Wann**

It's not necessary to memorize all of these rules right now. Learning some basic stock phrases will impress your hosts, friends and strangers. But if your aim is to actually begin to learn German, these rules will give you a structure that you can build on as you get a feel for the language and begin to fill in vocabulary and develop your listening skills.

Practice

Let's use the grammar rules and vocabulary you've learned so far to begin to create sentences. Remember, the more familiar you get with the structures now, the easier it will be to memorize the common phrases you'll use while traveling, follow conversations (because you won't spend so much time being confused about words being "in the wrong place"), and actually have conversations when you start developing the skills and vocabulary.

The girl has learned German.
Are you (informal) writing?
We had been drinking coffee.
The child has lost its (gender unknown) money.
The town has an old tree.
Where is my son?
Is this the family of the tall boy?
We drove until afternoon.
My brother bought a new cell phone from your business.
Their sister had seen a woman.
I bought a toy for my child.
Our room has a beautiful view.
Is their map under the table?
Did you meet my beautiful sister?

Chapter 6: Fundamental Vocabulary

Days of the Week

Monday	Montag	mahn'-tahk
Tuesday	Dienstag	deens'-tahk
Wednesday	Mittwoch	mit'-vokh
Thursday	Donnerstag	donners'-takh
Friday	Freitag	frī'-takh
Saturday	Samstag / Sonnabend	zoms'-takh/zōn'-abent
Sunday	Sonntag	zōn'-takh

Months

January	Januar	yah'-nuahr
February	Februar	feb'-ruahr
March	März	mairtz
April	April	ah-pril'
May	Mai	my
June	Juni	yoo'-nee
July	Juli	yoo'-lee
August	August	ow-goost
September	September	zept-em'-ber
October	Oktober	ok-tō'-ber
November	November	nō-vem'-ber
December	Dezember	day-tzem'-ber
monthly	monatlich	mō-naht'-likh
yearly	jährlich	jehr-likh

Time

What time is it?	Wie spät ist es?	vee shpāt ist es
It is...	Es ist...	es ist...
twelve o'clock	zwolf Uhr	tzvŏlf oor
two-fifteen	zwei Uhr fűnfzehn	tzvī oor fuenf'-tzān
three-thirty	drei Uhr dreißig	drī oor drī'-sik
four-forty-five	vier Uhr fűnfundvierzig	feer oor fuenf-unt-feer'-tzik
noon	Mittag	mit'-tak
midnight	Mitternacht	mit'-ter-nakht
this morning	heute Morgen	hoy'-tə mor'-gen
tonight	heute Abend	hoy'-tə ah'-bent
today	heute	hoy'-tə
tomorrow	morgen	mor'-gen
yesterday	gestern	gĕ'-stern
last night	letzter Nacht	letz-ter nokht
day after tomorrow	übermorgen	oo'-ber-mor-gen
next week	nächste Woche	nāsh'-tə vŏ-khə
next month	nächste Monat	nāsh'-tə mŏ'-not
last week	letzte Woche	letz-tə vŏ-khə
see you (until)...	bis...	biss

Chapter 7: Basic Phrases

Basic phrases are the fundamental building blocks of everyday language use. With the exceptions of individual letters and words, of course, they are the most important part of learning and speaking any language. Here we will delve into the some of the most common and useful phrases that the German language has to offer.

yes	ja	yah
no	nein	nīn
thank you	danke	dahnk-ə
thank you, too [in reply to "thank you" from someone else]	Ich danke Ihnen auch	ikh donk-ə een'-en oukh
please	bitte	bitt-ə
you're welcome	bitte schön	bit-tə shone
no problem	kein problem	kīn proh-blām'
excuse me; sorry	entschuldigung	ent-shuld'-igung
naturally; of course	natürlich	na-toor'-lish
correct	richtig	rikh'-tik
thank you very much	vielen dank	feel-en donk
no, thank you	nein, danke	nīn donk-ə
sorry (it gives me pain)	es tut mir leid	ess tüt meer lid
forgive me	verzeihen Sie	ver-tzī'-en zee
isn't that right?	nicht wahr	nikht var

Getting to Know You...

This section is comprised of phrases for use in casual conversations within the German vernacular.

(I am called...) My name is	**Ich heiße ...**	*ikh hīs-ə*
(informal) What is your name? (What are you called?)	**Wie heißt du?**	*vee hīst du*
(formal) What is your name?	**Wie heißen Sie?**	*vee hī'-sen zee*
(informal) Where are you from? (From where do you come?)	**Woher kommst du?**	*vo-hair comst du*
(formal) Where are you from? (From where do you come?)	**Woher kommen Sie?**	*vo-hair com'men zee*
I'm from...	**Ich komme aus...**	*ikh comm-ə ous*
(informal) I am happy to meet you.	**Nett dich kennenzulernen.**	*net dish ken'-nen-tzu-lair-nen*
(formal) I am happy to meet you.	**Nett Sie kennenzulernen.**	*nett zee ken'-nen-tzu-lair'nen*
(formal) Could I introduce you to...?	**Darf ich Ihnen . . . vorstellen?**	*Darf ikh <u>ee</u>-nen . . . <u>for</u>-shtêl-en*
My pleasure.	**Freut mich.**	*froyt mikh*
When is your birthday?	**Wann hast du Geburtstag?**	*von hast doo ge-boorts'-tak*
My birthday is in May.	**Mein Geburtstag ist im Mai.**	*mīn ge-boorts'-tak ist im mī*
(informal) Do you have children?	**Hast du Kinder?**	*hast doo kind'-er*
(formal) Do you have children?	**Habben Sie Kinder?**	*hab'-ben zee kind'-er*

(informal) Where do you live? (Where live you?)	**Wo wohnst du?**	*vō vōnst doo*
(formal) What place do you live at?	**Wo wohnen Sie?**	*vō vōn'-en zee*
My job is X.	**Ich bin X von Beruf.**	*ikh bin x fahn be-roof*
What do you normally do outside of work? (informal)	**Was machst du außerhalb der Arbeit?**	*vos mokhst doo ou-ser-holf dair ar'-bīt*
What are your activities outside of work? (formal)	**Was machen Sie außerhalb der Arbeit?**	*vos mokh-en zee ou-ser-holf dair ar'-bīt*
My hobbies are X, Y, and Z.	**Meine Hobbies sind X, Y, and Z.**	*mīn hobbies zint X, Y, unt Z*
I like to do X.	**Ich mache gerne X.**	*ikh makh-ə gern-ə X*
To get on with	**Auskommen Mit**	*Ows-komen met*
To describe	**Beschreiben**	*Besh-raben*
To go to sleep	**Einschlafen**	*In-Shlafen*
Love	**Liebe**	*Leeb*
To love	**Lieben**	*Leeb-n*
Part	**Teil**	*Tal*
To share	**Teilen**	*Tal-n*
Address	**Adresse**	*Address*
Age	**Alter**	*Al-tr*
Surname	**Brille**	*Bril*
Born	**Geboren**	*Ge-boar-en*
Birth (day/place of)	**Geburts (tag/ort)**	*Ge-brrts*
Home	**Heimat**	*Ha-mat*

Home journey/ Way home	**Heimfahrt/ Heimweg**	*H<u>a</u>m-fart/ Ham-weg*
To marry	**Heiraten**	*Har-<u>a</u>tin*
Single/ Unmarried	**Ledig**	*Lee-dig*
Dear (=letters)	**Leiber/ leibe**	*L<u>i</u>brr/ L<u>i</u>b*
Married	**Verheiratet**	*Fer-h<u>a</u>r-atet*
Engaged	**Verlobt**	*Fer-l<u>o</u>bt*
To promise	**Versprechen**	*Fer-spre-kin*
First name	**Vorname**	*For-nam*
Old (fashioned)	**Alt (modisch)**	*Alt (m<u>o</u>-deech)*
Pleasant/ Enjoyable	**Angenehm**	*An-ge-nem*
Famous	**Berhühmt**	*Brr-hoomt*

Small Talk

This section further explores words and phrases useful in getting to know another person in casual conversation.

(informal) How are you? (How does it go with you?)	**Wie geht es dir?**	*vee gāt es deer*
(formal) How are you? (How does it go with you?)	**Wie geht es Ihnen?**	*vee gāt es eenen*
(informal) Do you come here often?	**Kommst du oft hierher?**	*comst du oft here-hair*
(formal) Do you come here often?	**Kommen Sie oft hierher?**	*comen zee oft here-hair*
(informal) Can you speak English?	**Sprichst du Englisch?**	*shprikht du eng'-lish*
(formal) Can you speak English?	**Sprechen Sie Englisch?**	*shprekh-en zee eng'-lish*
I don't speak German (very well).	**Ich kann nicht (gut) Deutsch sprechen.**	*ikh con nikht zo goot doich shprekh'-en*
I can speak only a small amount of German.	**Ich spreche nur ein bisschen Deutsch.**	*ikh shprekh-ə noor īn bish-en doitsh*
I didn't understand.	**Ich verstehe nicht.**	*ikh vairshtay-ə nikht*
(informal) Would you mind repeating that?	**Kannst du das bitte weiderholen?**	*const du doss bitt-ə vee'-derholen*
(formal) Could you please say that again?	**Können Sie das bitte wiederholen?**	*cun'-nen zee doss bitt-ə vee'-der-hol-en*
(informal) Please say that again.	**Bitte, wiederholen.**	*bitt-ə vee'-der-hol-en*

(formal) Please say that again.	**Bitte, wiederholen Sie.**	*bitt-ə vee'-der-hol-en zee*
(informal) Could you please speak a little more slowly?	**Kannst du bitte langsamer sprechen?**	*const doo bitt-ə long'-zahm-er shprek'-en*
(formal) Could you please speak a little more slowly?	**Können Sie bitte langsamer sprechen?**	*cun-nen zee bitt-ə long'-zahm-er shprekh'-en*
What is X called in German?	**Wie heißt X auf Deutsch?**	*vee hīst x ouf doitsh*
How would someone say X in German?	**Wie sagt man X auf Deutsch?**	*vee zakt mon x ouf doitsh*
Would you translate that?	**Können Sie das übersetzen?**	*kun'-nen zee dos oo-ber-zet'-sen*
Thanks a lot for helping!	**Vielen Dank für Ihre Hilfe!**	*feel-en donk fyur eer-ə hilf-ə*
Do you understand? (informal)	**Verstehst du?**	*fair-shtāst doo*
Do you understand? (formal)	**Verstehen Sie?**	*fair-shtā'-en zee*
(informal) Please write that down for me.	**Schreibst du das bitte für mich auf.**	*shrī'-bst doo das bitt-ə fyur mikh ouf*
(formal) Please write that down for me.	**Schreiben Sie das bitte für mich auf.**	*shrī'-ben zee das bitt-ə fyur mikh ouf*
What does that mean?	**Was bedeutet das?**	*vas be-doy-tet das*
I don't know (I know not)	**ich weiß nicht**	*ikh vīs nikht*

all right	**in ordnung**	*in ordnung*
never mind	**macht nichts**	*makht nikhts*
How is the weather?	**Wie ist das Wetter?**	*vee ist dos vet'-er*
see you later	**bis später**	*biss shpāt'-er*
bye	**tschűß**	*shuss*
Take care!	**Machs gut!**	*mokhs goot*
See you!	**Bis dann!**	*bis dăn*
See you later! (Until later)	**Bis später!**	*bis shpāter*
See you soon! (Until soon)	**Bis gleich!**	*bis glīkh*
Get home safe!	**Komm gut nach hause!**	*kom goot nokh houz-ə*
Goodbye!	**Auf Wiedersehen!**	*ouf vee-der-zā'-en*
Have a nice day!	**Einen schönen Tag noch!**	*īn-en shō-nen tok nokh*
Have a good night!	**Gute Nacht!**	*goot-ə nokht*
Have a nice weekend!	**Schönes Wochenende!**	*shō'-nes vōkh'-en-en-də*
See you next time!	**Bis zum nächsten Mal!**	*bis tzoom nākh-sten mol*
Joy	**Freude**	*Froy-d*
Friendly	**Freundlich**	*Froynd-lik*
Awful	**Furchtbar**	*Furkt-bar*
Patient	**Geduldig**	*Ge-dul-dig*
To like	**Gefallen**	*Ge-fallen*
Tall	**Groß**	*Gross*
Size/ height (of a person)	**Größe**	*Grawss*
Helpful	**Hilfsbereit/ Hilfreich**	*Hillfs-berat/ Hill-frak*

Polite	**Höflich**	*Haw-flikh*
Pretty	**Hübsch**	*Hyub-skh*
Small/ short	**Klein**	*Kl<u>a</u>n*
Clever	**Klug**	*Kl<u>u</u>g*
Funny	**Komisch**	*Ko-mikh*
In a good/ bad mood	**Laune (Guter/ Schlechter)**	*Lawn (Goo-tr/ Shlekh-r)*
Noisey/ loud	**Laut**	*Lawt*
Curley	**Lockig**	*L<u>o</u>k-<u>i</u>g*
Tired/ tiring	**Müde/ ermüdend**	*Myud/ er-muydn-d*
Nice	**Nett**	*Net*
Tidy	**Ordentlich**	*Orden-likh*
Rich	**Reich**	*Raikh*
Clean	**Sauber**	*Saw-br*
Sharp	**Scharf**	*Sh-arf*
Slim	**Schlank**	*Shl-<u>a</u>nk*
Shy	**Schüchtern**	*Shyukh-ern*
Strong	**Stark**	*Stark*
Strict	**Streng**	*Streng*
Sad	**Traurig**	*Traw-rig*
Untidy	**Unordentlich**	*Un-orden-likh*
To understand (get on with)	**Verstehen (sich)**	*Fer-ste-hn (sikh)*

Shopping

This section is comprised of words and phrases that are useful to the native English speaker preparing to shop at any German-speaking establishment.

Some helpful tips for the foreigner shopping in Germany are as follows:

In German-speaking Europe (Germany, Switzerland, and Austria) it is never wise to assume that any given store or restaurant will accept credit and/or debit card payments. The culture prefers and appreciates cash to electronic payment methods.

Price tags in Germany already include the VAT (value-added tax). This includes sales tax, meaning that the price listed is what the buyer actually pays, unlike in America.

German-speaking nations are much more conservative in their shopping hours; in fact, Germany has a *Ladenschlußgesetz* (or store closing law) that prohibits businesses from remaining open for as long as the common store hours in lots of other countries.

In German supermarkets, there are typically far less brands to choose from than there are in American markets. One important thing for any foreigner about to shop for groceries in Germany is to remember to bring his or her own bag, as they are usually not free in German supermarkets.

And lastly, while there are lots of superstores in German-speaking Europe, there also happen to be lots of specialty stores as well. These stores are incredibly useful as their employees have more knowledge and information to provide customers than their counterparts at the superstores.

With that being said, below is a list of useful words and phrases for shopping in German-speaking countries.

English	German	Pronunciation
What would you like?	Was möchten Sie?	vos mush'-ten zee
What are you looking for?	Was suchen Sie?	vos zoo'-khen zee
Do you have...?	Haben Sie...?	hob-ben zee
Do you have souvenirs?	Haben Sie Andenken?	hob-ben zee on'-denk-en
Do you sell...?	Verkaufen Sie...?	fair-kouf'-en zee
Where do I find...?	Wo finde ich...?	vō find-ə ikh
Where is...?	Wo ist...?	vō ist
How much does that cost?	Wie viel kostet das?	vee feel costet dos?
Can I pay cash?	Kann ich bar bezahlen?	con ikh bar betzol'-en
Do you accept Visa/Mastercard?	Nehmen Sie Visa/Mastercard?	nām'-en zee Visa/Mastercard
Could I pay for this with a credit card?	Kann ich mit eine Kreditkarte zahlen?	con ikh mit credit-cart'-ə tzahl'-en
Where can I find a close ATM?	Wo ist der nächste Geldautomat?	vo ist dair nāsht-ə geld'-out-ō-mot
Can I buy it for X euros?	Kann ich es für X Euro kaufen?	con ikh ess fyoor x oorohz kouf'-en
Do you have something that costs less?	Haben Sie etwas Billigeres?	hob-ben zee etvas bill'-ə-gər-ess
Can I have a discount?	Können Sie mir darauf Rabatt geben?	kun-nen zee meer da-rouf ra-bot' gā-ben

Does that come in a [bigger/smaller] size?	Haben Sie das in einer [größeren/kleiner] Größe?	hob-ben zee doss in īn'-ər [klī'-ner/grōs'-er-en] grōs-ə
Could you wrap this as a present?	Können Sie das als Geschenk einpacken?	kun-nen zee dos als ge-shenk īn'-pok-en
What times does the shop [open/close]?	Um wieviel Uhr [öffnet/schließt] das Geschäft?	um vee-feel oor [uf'-net/shleest] doss ge-sheft
Where can I find the restrooms, please?	Wo sind die Toiletten, bitte?	vo zind dee toil-et'-ten bit-tə
Suit	Anzug	Ahn-zug
Bracelet (wristwatch)	Armband (uhr)	Arm-band (uhr)
Bra	BH/ Büstenhalter	BH/ Byust-n-hahltr
Blouse	Bluse	Bloos
Belt	Gürtel	Gyur-tel
Necklace	Halskette	Hahl-sket
Handbag	Handtasche	Hand-tash
Shirt	Hemd	Him-d
Trousers	Hose	Hoose
Hat	Hut	Hut
Jacket	Jacke	Jak
Dress	Kleid	Klade
Clothes/ Clothing	Kleider/ kleidung	Klad-r/ kla-dung
Tie	Krawatte/ schlips	Kra-waat
Coat	Mantel	Man-tl
Skirt	Rock	Rock
Pajamas	Schlafanzug	Shlaf-ahn-zoog
Shoes	Schuhe	Shoo
Sock	Socke	Sock
Boot	Stiefel	Stafl

Tights	**Strumpfhose**	*Strumpf-hoos*
To carry/ wear	**Tragen**	*Tra-gen*
Underpants	**Unterhose**	*Oontr-hoos*
Underwear	**Unterwäsche**	*Oontr-wowkh*
Towel (bath towel)	**Handtuch (badetuch)**	*Hand-tookh (bade-tookh)*
Radiator	**Heizkörper**	*Haz-Kirp-r*
Comb	**Kamm**	*Kahm*
Wardrobe	**Kleiderschrank**	*Kladr-shrank*
Lamp	**Lampe**	*Lamp*
Microwave	**Mikrowellenherd**	*Mikro-weln-herd*
Soap	**Seife**	*Safe*
Armchair	**Sessel**	*Ses-sl*
Sofa/ settee	**Sofa**	*Sofa*
Stereo system	**Stereoanlage**	*Stereo-an-lag*
Step/ stair	**Stufe**	*Stoof*
Chair	**Stuhl**	*Stool*
Tray	**Tablett**	*Tab-let*
Wallpaper	**Tapete**	*Tap-et*
Carpet	**Teppich**	*Te-pikh*
Freezer	**Tiefkühltruhe**	*Tef-kyul-tru*
Table	**Tisch**	*Tish*
Tablecloth	**Tischtuch**	*Tish-tukh*
Toiletpaper	**Toilettenpapier**	*Toilet-n-papier*
Saucepan	**Topf**	*Topf*
Cloth	**Tuch**	*Tukh*
Door	**Tür**	*Tyur*
Curtain	**Vorhang**	*For-hang*
Washing machine	**Waschmaschine**	*Vash-mach-ine*
Wash powder	**Waschpulver**	*Vash-pol-fr*
Tap	**Wasserhahn**	*Vassr-han*
Alarm clock	**Wecker**	*Vek-r*

Getting Around

This section may prove to be the most useful for anyone travelling in any German-speaking land, as it is filled with a wide variety of very useful words and phrases that pertain to travelling.

Germany is a much frequented hotspot for travellers from all corners of the globe. Known for their austere work ethic and remarkable efficiency, the German people know how to make a nation welcoming and agreeable. One of Germany's most remarkable characteristics is how effortless the medieval intertwines with the contemporary. Stepping onto the German countryside for the first time is at once like entering an ancient fairytale, and a futuristic Asimovian wonderland. If the former, with its dense forests and pristine lakes and rivers don't sound like your ideal vacation spot, then the latter may be more your taste, with everything modernity has to offer.

There are, however, a few things the average traveller needs to know before entering Germany.

First of all, Germany is a European Union state. This means that they use the Euro as currency, among other things. Germany also happens to be a signatory of the Schengen convention. With this being said, any given national of the EU has a right to unlimited and free travel within Germany. Nationals from other western countries are, on the other hand, only entitled to 90 days of unrestricted travel with Germany. Beyond that 90 day threshold a Schengen visa is required for further stay. Nationals of most eastern countries, however, have the harshest restrictions; they have to acquire a Schengen visa to travel to Germany in the first place.

Another aspect of German culture that is very much appreciable is that it's relatively safe. With a low crime rate and virtually no natural disasters, Germany is generally much safer than lots of western nations. It is always advisable though, to err on the side of safety, to invest in travel insurance, no matter where one travels.

The intrepid traveler may or may not find it hard to nail down a time of year to visit Germany. While this is, of course, a matter of personal preference, it is generally believed that Germany is a nation that is best to be explored during the summer months.
To that end, every time of year in Germany produces its own charms. The so-called 'low' season (Nov-Mar) has the coldest weather. Ski resorts, theater, concerts, and opera are most popular during this season.

The 'mid' seasons (Apr-Jun, Sep-Oct) brings nice, mild weather and, with it, lower prices.

And finally the 'high' season (Jul and Aug) brings the best weather as well as the most energy and activity. The highest prices and the most congestion are also to be expected within this season though.

Another significant aspect to consider when travelling to this nation is, of course, the expenses involved. While Germany is not the cheapest nation to visit, there still are numerous ways to travel the land without bankrupting one's self. In fact, according to one estimate, it is possible to visit Germany for as little 40-80 US dollars a day.
Some price estimates for travelling expenses in Germany are listed below:

Accommodation:
€10-30 ($12-35) dorms
€45-65 ($50-75) budget hotels
      Mid-Range: €60-100 ($70-120)
      Splurge: €150+ ($175+)

Food (meals for one):
Street food: €2-4 ($2-5)
Cheap meal at beer hall: €9-15 ($11-18)
Restaurant: €15-20 ($18-25)
Top-rated restaurant: €100 ($115)

Transportation:
Bike Rental: €18 ($21) per day
City Transit: €1-3 ($1-4) per single ticket
Intercity Bus: €15-30 ($18-35)
Overnight buses: €20-70 ($25-82)
Trains: €40-70 ($48-82) slow
      €100+ ($120+) high-speed

As you can probably see, Germany is not only not as expensive to travel to, as the average person would guess it is, but it is, in fact, even cheaper to travel to than lots of US cities. Take New York, Boston, San Diego, and Washington D.C. for example, their average nightly rates for hotels range from $250-$370. These figures seem almost ludicrous when compared to the $70-$175 of most German cities. To add to that, the traveller is getting the added historical value of a handful of more than 1,000-year-old buildings in Germany, so to say the least, the educational and cultural value of a trip to Germany just can't be rivaled by a trip to many American cities.

When packing one's suitcase for Germany, it is important to include a wide variety of articles of clothing. The weather is rather fickle in Germany, and in every season, too; so it is best to come prepared for whatever weather mother nature has to offer.

Berlin, the capital of Germany, has a well-deserved reputation as being a great city for freelancers and otherwise creative people—with its world famous nightlife, art, museums, cafe culture, and music scene. It is also widely known for its interesting historical significance.

The demeanor of *Munich* is more staid and quieter, with the exception of its annual celebration of Oktoberfest. It holds historical buildings, museums, parks, and popular beer halls all side by side.

While Berlin and Munich are both enchanting and becoming cities, we would be remiss to not pour over some of the other great cities Germany has to offer. These include *Hamburg*, famous for its parks, canals, and boasting the second busiest port in Europe. *Frankfurt* is a city better suited for the history and or science lover. It has a number of historical sites, science museums, and a famous restaurant scene. *Cologne* is another city well suited for the history lover. It has historical sites including its world famous cathedral. And finally, for those who want a fine mixture of modernity and nature, *Dresden* is a great city to find that balance.

One aspect of travel in Germany that is—more often than not—neglected by visitors, and also of travelers in any part of the globe, for that matter, is the natural landscapes the countryside has to offer. Germany has no shortage of natural wonders, and there are many places that a traveler can go to witness just what the country really has to offer. One spot in Germany that's perfect for those who love the outdoors is *Berchtesgaden*

National Park. It is known for its dense forests, clear lakes, and huge boulders. *Lake Constance*, the largest freshwater lake in Germany, may also be a better fit for the outdoorsman.

One of the finest forests in Germany is the *Black Forest*. It is located in a mountainous region in southwest Germany, bordering France. This forest is widely known for the abundance of its megaflora and the archaic, charming villages nestled within its dense interior. This is a great spot for a slower paced vacation in a natural setting.

One cannot mention travel within Germany without a talking about the castles and palaces that inhabit the land. One of the most famous examples of these, forever memorialized by the Disney Corporation and by its architecture in and of itself, is *Neuschwanstein Castle.* This is one of the more intriguing and impressive buildings the globe has to offer and nothing can really supplement seeing it in person, so trekking to this building would be an unassailably important part of any vacation to Germany.

While the Germans, being sensible people, often speak English, (so often, in fact, that English is a mandatory subject for many of Germany's students from the fifth grade onward) the list below should still prove to be of great help for the foreigner as it includes lots of words and phrases useful in travelling.

Where?	**Wo?**	*vō*
I need some information.	**Ich brauche eine Auskunft**	*ikh broukh-ə īnə ous'-kunft*
I need help.	**Ich brauche Hilfe.**	*ikh broukh-ə hilf-ə*
Do you know the area?	**Kennen Sie sich hier aus?**	*ken'-nen zee zikh heer ous*
Am I in the right place?	**Bin ich hier richtig?**	*bin ikh heer rikh'-tik*

Excuse me, where is…?	**Entschuldigung, wo ist…?**	*ent-shul'-dĭ-gung vō ist*
Which direction is X in?	**In welcher Richtung ist X?**	*in vel'-kher rĭkh'-tung ist x*
Where is the [entrance/exit]?	**Wo ist der [Eingang/Ausgang]?**	*vō ist dare [īn'-gong/ous'-gong]*
Where is the bus stop?	**Wo ist die Bushaltestelle?**	*vō ist dee boos-halt'-ə-shtell-ə*
Where is the underground train (subway/metro)?	**Wo ist die U-Bahn?**	*vō ist dee oo'-bon*
One ticket to …, please!	**Eine Fahrkarte nach …, bitte!**	*īn-ə farcart-ə bitt- ə*
When does the next train for … leave?	**Wann fährt der nächste Zug nach …?**	*von fairt dair nāshte tzug nosh*
Where does is this bus going to?	**Wohin fährt dieser Bus?**	*vohin fairt deezer bus*
When is this train scheduled to arrive?	**Wann kommt dieser Zug an?**	*von comt deezer tzug on*
I wonder where this bus goes to?	**Fährt dieser Bus nach…?**	*fairt deezer bus nokh*
Could I please have a map of the city?	**Darf ich bitte einen Stadtplan haben?**	*darf ikh bitt-ə shtot'-plon hobb-en*
Please take me to this address.	**Bringen Sie mich bitte zu dieser Adresse.**	*bring-en zee mikh bitt-ə tzoo deez-er ad-res-sə*
I am looking for the museum/park/hote	**Ich suche das Museum/den**	*ikh zookh-ə dos moo-zā-əm/dān*

l.	**Park/das Hotel.**	*park/dos hō-tel*
Please stop here.	**Halten Sie bitte hier an.**	*holt-en zee bitt-ə heer on*
To the city center, please.	**Zum Stadtzentrum, bitte.**	*tzoom shtat-tzen'-troom bit-tə*
To the train station, please.	**Zum Bahnhof, bitte.**	*tzoom bon-hof bit-tə*
To the airport, please.	**Zum Flughafen, bitte.**	*tzoom floog'-hof-en*
Where is a good bakery?	**Wo ist eine leckere Bäckerei?**	*vō ist ī-nə lĕk'-er-ə bĕk'-er-ī*
Where is a close gas station?	**Wo ist die nächste Tankstelle?**	*vō ist der nākh'-stə tonk'-shtell-ə*
At what place is the bank?	**Wo ist die Bank?**	*vō ist dee bahnk*
Is the airport far away?	**Ist der Flughafen weit weg?**	*ist der floog'-haf-fen vīt vek*
I would like to be shown?	**Können Sie mir das zeigen?**	*cunn-en zee meer doss tzī'-gən*
Do I have to change?	**Muss ich umsteigen?**	*moos ikh um-shtī'-gən*
It's there. / There it is.	**Es ist da. / Da ist es.**	*ess ist dah/dah ist ess*
around the corner	**um die Ecke**	*um dee ĕ-kə*
to the left	**nach links**	*nokh linx*
to the right	**nach rechts**	*nakh rekhs*
straight ahead	**geradaus**	*ger-ah'-dous*
upstairs	**oben**	*ō'-ben*
downstairs	**unten**	*un'-ten*
back	**zurück**	*tzoo-rook'*
north	**Nord**	*nord*

south	**Süd**	*zoot*
east	**Ost**	*ōst*
West	**West**	*vest*
Brochure	**Broschüre**	*Broschüre*
Campsite	**Campingplatz**	*Campingplatz*
Reception(ist)	**Empfang(sdame)**	*Empfang(sdame)*
Holiday	**Ferien**	*Ferien*
Lost Property Office	**Fundbüro**	*Fundbüro*
Guest	**Gast**	*Gast*
Host	**Gastgeber**	*Gastgeber*
Restaurant/ Pub	**Gaststätte**	*Gaststätte*
Luggage	**Gepäck**	*Gepäck*
Map	**Landkarte**	*Landkarte*
Place	**Ort**	*Ort*
Passport	**Pass (reisepass)**	*Pass (reisepass)*
Identity Card	**Personalausweis**	*Personalausweis*
Traveller	**Reisende(r)**	*Reisende(r)*
Destination	**Reiseziel**	*Reiseziel*
Cheque Book	**Scheckheft**	*Scheckheft*
Sleeping Bag	**Schlafsack**	*Schlafsack*
To stay the night	**übernachten**	*übernachten*
Accomodation	**Unterkunft**	*Unterkunft*
Maid	**Zimmermädchen**	*Zimmermädchen*
Overcast	**Bedeckt**	*Bee-dekt*
To thunder	**Donnern**	*Don-uhrn*
Dark	**Dunkel**	*Dun-kel*
To freeze	**Frieren**	*Fri-rn*
Thunderstorm	**Gewitter**	*Ge-wit-r*

Hail	**Hagel**	*Hagl*
Hot	**Heiß**	*Hass*
Heat	**Hitze**	*Hit-z*
Cold	**Kalte**	*Kahlt*
Climate	**Klima**	*Klim-ah*
Cool	**Kühl**	*Kyuhl*
Wet	**Nass**	*Nass*
Fog(gy)/ Mist(y)	**Nebel (nebelig)**	*Ne-bel (ne-bel-ig)*
Rain(coat)	**Regen (mantel)**	*Re-gen (mant-l)*
Umbrella	**Regenschirm**	*Re-gen-shirm*
To rain	**Regnen**	*Reg-nen*
To shine	**Scheinen**	*Shan-en*
Snow	**Schnee**	*Shn-ee*
To snow	**Schneien**	*Shnen*
Sun	**Sonne**	*Son*
Sunny	**Sonnig**	*Son-ig*
Stormy	**Sturm/ Stürmisch**	*Sturm/ Styur-mish*
Weather (forecast)	**Wetter (bericht/ vorhersage)**	*Vet-r (b-rikh/ vor-hr-sage)*
Cloud (less)	**Wolke (wolkenlos)**	*Vohlk (Vohlk-n-los)*

Lodging & Hotels

This one relates to the previous section in its utility for travellers.

The words and phrases listed below are useful to anyone lodging in any German-speaking areas.

Are there any available rooms?	**Sind noch Zimmer frei?**	*zint noch tzimmer frī*
What does a double room cost?	**Wie viel kostet ein Doppelzimmer?**	*vee feel cost'-et īn dop'-pel-tzim-mer*
What does a single room cost?	**Wie viel kostet ein Einzelzimmer?**	*vee feel costet īn īn'-tzel-tzim-mer*
When is breakfast?	**Wann gibt es Frühstück?**	*von gibt ess froo'-shtook/ah-bent-es-sen*
Does this room come with ...? (Has this room...)	**Hat das Zimmer ...?**	*Hot dos tzim'-mer*
balcony	**einen Balkon**	*īn-en bol-cone'*
television	**einen Fernseher**	*īn-en fairn'-zā-er*
WiFi	**Wifi**	*vī-fi*
air conditioning	**eine Klimaanlage**	*īn-ə clee'-mon-lag-ə*
I'm staying for ... night.	**Ich bleibe für ... Nacht.**	*ikh blīb'-ə fyur... nakht*
one night	**eine Nacht**	*īn'-ə nokht*
three nights	**drei Nächte**	*drī někht'-ə*
I would like a room.	**Ich hätte gern ein Zimmer.**	*ikh hět-tə gairn īn tzim-mer*
I will stay for [one night/two	**Ich bleibe [eine Nacht/zwei**	*ikh blīb [īn-ə nokht/tzwī někht-*

nights/three nights].	**Nächte/drei Nächte].**	*ə/drī někht-ə*
Is breakfast included?	**Ist Frühstück inklusiv?**	*ist froo'-shtook in'-kloos-eef*
Would you please wake me up at 8 o'clock?	**Können Sie mich um acht Uhr wecken?**	*Kun-nen zee mikh um x oor věk'-en*
room service	**Zimmerdienst**	*tzim'-mer-deenst*
shower	**Dusche**	*doosh*
single room	**Einzelzimmer**	*īn'-tzel-tzim-mer*
air conditioning	**Klimaanlage**	*kleem-a-ahn'-lag-ə*
key	**Schlüssel**	*shloo'-sel*

Eating Out

There are lots of mannerisms that differentiate German dining from dining in other countries. Featured below is a short list of these mannerisms useful for anyone not familiar with the German dining experience:

Upon entering a restaurant in German-speaking Europe, it is not advisable to wait to be seated. It is generally expected of diners to find tables on their own. Servers seldom suggest tables to incoming diners because they are usually busy with current diners. Unless the diner sees the words spelled out: 'please wait to be seated,' he or she should find his or her own seat.

Most Americans have come to expect a glass of water with every meal that they eat out. Most Europeans, on the other hand, avoid drinking tap water with any of their meals, not out of concern for safety or hygiene, but because they don't like the idea of having such a bland liquid with their food. They prefer to diversify with their drinks.

If water is requested, it is only rarely tap water, but usually *mineralwasser* (or mineral water) instead. Americans requesting tap water at public eateries in Europe are usually met with looks of disgust. Mineral water is the preferred drink.

Germans are known for having a very practical and also very amiable custom of sitting with the strangers around them while eating at their beer gardens and restaurants, where long tables and numerous empty seats are common.

Bread rolls are other extras that are usually not free in Germany, or most of Europe for that matter. While they are supposedly free in America, they are often still included in the price of the full meal, so the only difference in this European custom is its relative honesty and straightforwardness.

À la carte dining is the most common type of purchase in German-speaking Europe. Usually, any given side dishes are ordered and paid for independently of the main course that the diner chooses. In short, a diner pays only for what he or she consumes in Germany, which can be either very beneficial or detrimental to him or her.

That, in turn, brings us now to the all-important topic of payment in German dining.
As is common in America, the payments and tipping for meals in German-speaking Europe are both done at the table eaten at, and the server commonly carries a money pouch holstered around his or her waist as the work is done. However, unlike in America, the checks always have to be requested after a meal. Servers don't bring them about until they are.

The average and righteous tipping amount in Germany is +- 15%, as is the case in America, but tips are and should never be left on the table. As is the case in America, it is not required that any given diner tips his or her server, but it is also generally frowned upon when a diner is remiss to reward a server's good work. Another fact that also shares similitude with American dining is the fact that servers in Germany live meagerly off of mostly tips, and that it is very important that they are rewarded for their work.
When paying with a credit card in Germany, the tipping process is slightly different than it is in America. The diner typically is required to tell the server the amount of the tip before the card is swiped. It is, of course, always ideal to pay the tip in cash, as the server doesn't have to pay income taxes on cash tips.

As was mentioned before, sales tax is included in the price of nearly everything purchased in Germany before the transaction. This sales tax is fairly high, however, at 19%.

Another point that has been mentioned is the fact that many German stores do not accept credit cards. Unfortunately for most Americans who live and die by electronic currencies, the same is true for many German restaurants of all tiers. This is why it is wise to ask about electronic payments before ordering.

Now that we know some important points on dining in Germany, it may also be helpful to go over some of what the German cuisine includes.

Next to some of its European neighbors (such as Italy, or France, or Spain just to name a few) Germany's cuisine may seem boring or even unappetizing to many foreigners, but nothing could be further from the truth. Their food has, however, built up quite a well-deserved reputation for its hardiness and the relative simplicity of its recipes. But, for whatever one's palate desires, there is sure to be a German dish willing and ready to meet any given needs.

The first food to be mentioned is a very famous one in the US, and all throughout the world for that matter. It is the *bratwürst*. This is a remarkably popular German sausage, the best of which supposedly come from Nürnberg. These are usually made from pork shoulder, veal shoulder, pork fat, and spices.

Another very popular German dish goes by the name of *spätzle*. This is a vegetarian (rare in German cuisine) pasta dish consisting of eggs, flour, salt, and water. Like any pasta, it is best served as a side or a compliment to another dish. It is also good when served with cheese alone. Again, the beauty of some of Germany's greatest food lies within their simplicity.

But any discussion surrounding German pastas cannot be complete without the mention of *maultaschen*. This is a great ravioli dish which can be compared to a hot pocket. It can be, and usually is, stuffed with minced meat, sauerkraut, spinach, or really any other food for that matter. They can also be boiled or fried, and served as a main dish or as a side dish. They are great no matter how the diner takes them.

And lastly, also perhaps most famously, we come to the *bretzel*, or pretzel in English. One feature of the German *bretzel* that distinguishes it from its American cousin is its robustness. This is a classic snack food that can be found at fairs, carnivals, sporting events, virtually any public happening across the globe, and for good reason.

And now that we have been over German dining and some of the nation's foods, we can
at last come to some vocabulary over German dining:

Are you hungry? (informal)	**Hast du Hunger?**	*host doo hun-ger*
Are you hungry? (formal)	**Haben Sie Hunger?**	*hob'-ben zee hun-ger*
Are you thirsty? (informal)	**Hast du Durst?**	*host doo durst*
Are you thirsty? (formal)	**Haben Sie Durst?**	*hob'-ben zee durst*
Shall we get something to eat/drink	**Wollen wir etwas zusammen essen/trinken**	*vol-len veer et-vos tzoo-sam'-men es-sen/trink-*

together?	**gehen?**	*en gā-en*
Breakfast	**Frühstück**	*froo'-shtook*
Lunch	**Mittagessen**	*mitt'-ak-es-sen*
Dinner	**Abendessen**	*ah'-bent-es-sen*
A table for one/two/three…, please.	**Einen Tisch für eine Person/zwei/drei …, bitte.**	*ī' nen tish fyur īn-ĕ pair-zōn/tzvī/drī… bitt'-ə*
A menu, please.	**Die Speisekarte, bitte.**	*dee shpī'-zə-cart-ə, bitt-ə*
Waiter! / Waitress!	**Kellner!/Kellnerin!**	*kell'-ner/kell'-ner-in*
I'd like….	**Ich hätte gern….**	*ikh hêt-ə gern*
I'd like….	**Ich möchte gern….**	*ikh mukht-ə gern*
Nothing for me, thank you.	**Für mich nichts, danke.**	*fyur mikh nikhts donk-ə*
Would you recommend something?	**Könnten Sie etwas empfehlen?**	*kun-ten zee êt-vas êmp-fā'-len*
I only eat vegetables.	**Ich bin Vegetarier.**	*ikh bin vā'-gə-tair-ier*
Do you have food for vegetarians?	**Haben Sie vegetarisches Essen?**	*hobben zee vā-gə-tair'-ish-ess ess-en*
Is that gluten-free?	**Ist das glutenfrei?**	*ist dos gloot'-en-frī*

I am allergic to X.	**Ich bin allergisch gegen X.**	*ikh bin all-er-gish gā-gen X*
Nuts	**Nusse**	*noo-sə*
Shellfish	**Schalentiere**	*shol-en-teer'-ə*
Dairy	**Milch**	*Milkh*
Strawberries	**Erdbeeren**	*aird-beer'-en*
Gluten	**Gluten**	*gloot'-en*
Okay, I will take that.	**Gut, das nehme ich.**	*goot, dos nā-mə ikh*
I'd like to have some X please.	**Ich hätte gerne X.**	*ikh hĕt-tə gern-ə X*
Chicken	**Hühnchen**	*hoon'-shyen*
Pork	**Schweinefleisch**	*shvīn'-ə-flīsh*
Beef	**Rindfleisch**	*rĭnd'-flīsh*
Soup	**Suppe**	*zoop'-ə*
Pasta	**Nudeln**	*nood'-eln*
Vegetables	**Gemüse**	*ge-myooz'-ə*
Spicy	**scharf**	*sharf*
Sweet	**süß**	*soos*
Sour	**sauer**	*sou'-er*
Salt	**Salz**	*Zoltz*

Pepper	**Pfeffer**	*feff'-ər*
Sugar	**Zucker**	*tzoo'-kər*
Napkin	**Serviette**	*ser-vee-et'*
Plate	**Teller**	*tell'-er*
Fork	**Gabel**	*go'-bel*
Spoon	**Löffel**	*luff'-əl*
knife	**Messer**	*mess'-ər*
Glass	**Glas**	*glos*
Cup	**Tasse**	*toss'-ə*
Beer	**Bier**	*beer*
Wine	**Wein**	*vīn*
tap water	**Leitungswasser**	*lī'-tungs-voss-er*
A glass of water, please.	**Ein Glas Wasser, bitte.**	*īn glos voss'-ər bitt-ə*
[Sparkling/not sparkling], please.	**[Mit/ohne] Sprudel, bitte.**	*[mit/ōn-ə] shproo'-dl bit-tə*
A beer please!	**Ein Bier bitte!**	*īn beer bit-tə*
What's on tap?	**"Was gibt's vom Fass?"**	*vos gibts vom fos*
With lactose-free milk, please.	**Mit laktosefreier Milch, bitte.**	*mit lak'-tōs-frī-ər milkh bitt-ə*

Another one, please!	**Noch eine, bitte!**	*nokh īn'-ə bit-ə*
Another of the same, please.	**Das Gleiche nochmal bitte.**	*dos glīkh nokh-mol bit-tə*
Can I get that without tomato?	**Kriege ich das auch ohne Tomaten?**	*kreeg-ə ikh dos oukh ō-nə tō-mot-ten*
Do you have dessert too?	**Gibt's auch Nachtisch?**	*gibts oukh nokh-tish*
Can you wrap that up to go?	**Können Sie das einpacken?**	*kun-nen zee dos īn'-pok-en*
That was delicious!	**Das hat hervorragend geschmeckt!**	*dos hot hair-for'-ra-gent ge-shmekt*
One coffee, please!	**Einen Kaffee bitte!**	*īn-en kof-fā bit-tə*
Excuse me please.	**Entschuldigen Sie bitte.**	*ênt-shool'-də-gen zee bit-tə*
Could you show me to the restroom?	**Wo ist die Toilette?**	*vō isst dee toy-lett'-ə*
men	**Herren/Männer**	*hair'-en/měn'-ər*
women	**Damen/Frauen**	*dah'-men/frou'-en*
I am full.	**Ich bin satt.**	*ikh bin zot*
Please bring the check.	**Die Rechnung bitte.**	*dē rêkh-nung bitt-ə*

A receipt, please.	**Eine Quittung bitte.**	īn-ə kvĭ'-tung bitt-ə
Could I get a receipt, please?	**Darf ich eine Quittung haben, bitte?**	darf ikh īn-ə kvĭ'-tung bitt-ə
Enjoy. (Good appetite)	**Guten Appetit.**	goo-ten âp-ə-tēt'
Cheers!	**Zum Wohl!**	tzoom vōl
Cheers!	**Prost!**	Prōst
Flame	**Flamme**	Fl<u>a</u>mme
Bottle	**Flasche**	Fl<u>a</u>sh
Fresh	**Frisch**	Fr<u>i</u>sh
Dish/ Course	**Gericht**	Jer<u>i</u>-kt
Jar/ Pot	**Glas**	Glass
To grill/ Barbeque	**Grillen**	Grill-an
Snack (bar)	**Imbiss (stube)**	Em-b<u>i</u>ss (stoo<u>b</u>)
Canteen	**Kantine**	K<u>a</u>n-teen
Kitchen	**Küche**	Koo-ch
Delicious	**Lecker**	Le-kerr
Spoon	**Löffel**	Law-fell
Meal	**Mahlzeit**	M<u>a</u>ll-zat
Knife	**Messer**	Mes-ser

Dessert	**Nachtisch**	*N<u>a</u>k-tish*
To taste	**Schmecken**	*Shm<u>e</u>k-in*
Fast-food Restaurant	**Schnellimbiss**	*Shnel-l<u>i</u>m-biss*
Bowl	**Schüssel**	*Shoo-sell*
Self-service	**Selbstbedienung**	*Selbst-b<u>e</u>die-nung*
Menu	**Speisekarte**	*Sp<u>ace</u>-kart*
Supermarket	**Supermarkt**	*Super-market*

Emergencies

This section is one of great utility not only for German language learners, but also for anyone who may have friends or relatives who speak only German. It is a list of words and phrases useful in emergency or crisis situations.

help	**hilfe**	*hilf-ə*
fire	**feuer**	*foy'-er*
(informal) Call the police!	**Ruf die Polizei!**	*roof dee po-leet-zī'*
Stop! A thief!	**Halt! Ein Dieb!**	*halt īn deeb*
I am getting sick.	**Ich bin krank.**	*ikh bin kronk*
I don't feel too well.	**Mir geht es nicht so gut.**	*meer gāt es nikht zō goot*
She has gotten sick.	**Sie ist krank geworden.**	*zee ist kronk ge-vor'-den*
He needs a doctor.	**Er braucht einen Arzt.**	*air broucht īn'-en artst*

Where's the closest hospital?	**Wo ist das nächste Krankenhaus?**	*vō ist doss nāshte cron'-ken-hous*
My wallet has been lost.	**Ich habe mein Portemonnaie verloren.**	*ikh hobb-ə mīn port-e-mon-ī'] fair-lor'-en*
Someone took my bag.	**Jemand hat meine Tasche genommen.**	*yā'-mont hot mīn-ə tosh'-ə ge-nō'-men*
Where is the hospital?	**Wo ist das Krankenhaus?**	*vō ist dos kronk'-en-hous*
Where is the pharmacy?	**Wo ist die Apotheke?**	*vō ist dē ah-pō-tāk'*
Do you have aspirin?	**Haben Sie Aspirin?**	*hobb-en zee asp-ir-in*
This is an emergency.	**Es ist ein Notfall.**	*ess ist īn nōt'-fol*
I am lost.	**Ich habe mich verlaufen.**	*ikh hob-ə mikh fer-louf'-en*

Holiday Greetings

Public holidays in Germany, along with their celebrations, differ from state to state. While the most common christian holidays of the western world are celebrated eagerly in each and every state in Germany, there is still variance in the celebration of more minor holidays from state to state.

Major holidays which are celebrated in every state in Germany (Baden-Wüttemberg, Bavaria, Berlin, Brandenburg, Bremen, Hamburg, Hesse, Mecklenburg-Vorpommern, Lower Saxony, North Rhine-Westphalia, Rhineland-Palatinate, Saarland, Saxony, Saxony-Anhalt, Schleswig-Holstein, and Free State of Thuringia) are listed below:

- *New Year's Day* (Neujahrstag)
- *Good Friday* (Karfreitag)
- *Easter Monday* (Ostermontag)
- *Labour Day* (Tag Der Arbeit)
- *Ascension Day* (Christi Himmelfahrt)
- *White Monday* (Pfingstmontag)
- *German Unity Day* (Tag Der Deutschen Einheit)
- *Christmas Day* (Weihnachtstag)
- *St. Stephen's Day/ Boxing Day* (Zweiter Weihnachtsfeiertag)

More minor holidays which are not necessarily and officially celebrated in every state, but are still important days of the German year are listed below:

- *Epiphany* (Heilige Drei Könige)
- *Corpus Christi* (Fronleichnam)
- *Peace Festival* (Friedensfest)
- *Assumption Day* (Mariä Himmelfahrt)

- *Reformation Day* (Reformationstag)
- *All Saints Day* (Allerheiligen)
- *Repentance and Prayer Day* (Buß- und Bettag)

Of all the holidays previously mentioned, a small number of them are known as *stille tage* (or quiet days). On these days, louder public functions, such as public dancing events, public concerts, music at inns, etc., are prohibited by law.

These holidays are as follows:

Good Friday, Repentance and Prayer Day, All Saints Day, Memorial Day, Totensonntag, Christmas Eve, Ash Wednesday, Holy Thursday, Holy Saturday, All Souls Day.
Another category of holiday in Germany is that of the Flag Days (or Beflaggung Stage).

While the highest of governmental facilities are required to show their flags on every day of each year, on the days listed below, flag showing is required by federal decree for everyone:

Holocaust Memorial Day, Labor Day, Europe Day, Constitution Day, Remembrance of June 17th, World Refugee Day, Remembrance of July 20th, German Unity Day, Memorial Day (half-mast), and Election Day.

In addition to the official public holidays previously mentioned, there are a small number of unofficial German holidays that are worthy of note.

These are as follows:

Carnival Monday (or Mardis Gras as it is known throughout many parts of the US and other parts of the globe) traditionally starts on 11/11 at 11.11 am.

Presently, Christmas Eve has been becoming more of its own holiday than not, as it is more and more uncommon to work on that day and schools are always closed.

This is another section that is useful not only for German language learners, but anyone who knows German speakers and wants to wish them happy holidays.

Happy birthday!	**Herzlichen Glückwunsch zum Geburtstag!**	*hairtz'-lich-en glook'-vunsh tzoom ge-boorts-tok*
Merry Christmas!	**Frohe Weihnachten!**	*frō'-ə vī'-nach-ten*
Happy New Year!	**Frohes Neues!**	*frō'-ə noy'-ess*
Happy Easter!	**Frohe Ostern!**	*frō'-ə ō'-stern*
Congratulations!	**Herzliche Glückwünsche!**	*hairtz'-likh-ə glook'-voonsh-ə*
New Year's Day	**Neujahrstag**	*Noo-jahr-staag*
Good Friday	**Karfreitag**	*Kaar-fra-tag*
Easter Monday	**Ostermontag**	*Oostr-mon-tag*
Labor Day	**Tag Der Arbeit**	*Tag-dr-rbat*
Ascension Day	**Christi Himmelfahrt**	*Kristi Himel-fart*
White Monday	**Pfingstmontag**	*fingst-mon-tag*
German Unity Day	**Tag Der Deutschen Einheit**	*Tag dr dooych-n in-hat*
Christmas Day	**Weihnachtstag**	*Vah-nacht-stag*
St. Stephen's Day/ Boxing Day	**Zweiter Weihnachtsfeiertag**	*sva-tr vah-nachts-faer-tag*
Epiphany	**Heilige Drei Könige**	*Ha-lig dri kyon-ig*
Corpus Christi	**Fronleichnam**	*Fron-lach-nam*
Peace Festival	**Friedensfest**	*Frad-ns-fest*

Assumption Day	**Mariä Himmelfahrt**	*Maria himl-fart*
Reformation Day	**Reformationstag**	*Re-form-ation-stag*
All Saints Day	**Allerheiligen**	*Alr-hali-gen*
Repentance and Prayer Day	**Buß- und Bettag**	*Bus und beet-ag*

Chapter 8: Putting it All Together

Basic Conversations

An informal introduction might go something like this:
- **Das ist mein Freund**(m)/**meine Freundin**(f)...
  (dos ist mī-ne friyn-den/mīn froint)
  (This is my friend...)
- **Hallo, es freut mich dich kennenzulernen.**
  (Hallo, es froit mikh dikh kennenzulairnen)
  (Hello, it's nice to meet you.)
        OR
- **Freut mich.**
  (froit mikh)
  (Pleased to meet you.)
- **Mich auch.**
  (mikh oukh)
  (Me too.)

If the situation calls for a more formal introduction, you might say (or hear) this:
- **Guten Abend! Darf ich Ihnen... vorstellen?**
  (goot-en o-bent darf ikh ee-nen... for-shtel-en)
  (May I introduce you...?)
- **Freut mich Sie kennenzulernen.**
  (froit mikh zee ken'-nen-tzu-lern-nen)
  (Pleased to make your acquaintance.)
- **Meinerseits./Ganz meinerseits.**
  (mī-ner-zīts)/(gǎntz mī-ner-zīts)
  (Me too.)

"Likewise" is not the actual translation of the German word **"meinerseits." Meinerseits** literally means "mine." **Ganz**

meinerseits literally means "all mine," as in, "the pleasure is all mine."

The conversation might continue in a similar vein:

- **Ist der Platz noch frei?**
  (ist der plots nokh frī)
  (Is this seat still free?)
- **Ja, bitte.**
  (yah, <u>bit</u>-tə)
  (Yes, please.)

"Please" is used slightly more loosely in German than in English. You might think of it as "Please feel free" in this case.

This conversation would be very different among younger people at a party or some other informal setting.

- **Wie heißt du?**
  (vee hīst doo)
  (What's your name?)
- **Ich heiße _____. Und du?**
  (ikh hīs-sə _____. unt doo)
  (I am called _____. And you?)
- **_____. Wer ist das?**
  (ver ist dos)
  (_____. Who is that?)
- **Das ist meine Freundin _____.**
  (dos ist <u>mī</u>-nə <u>froin</u>-din)
  (This is my friend _____.)

Chapter 9: Continuing to Learn

The German language is a beautiful and elegant tongue. Learning a new language is never easy, but if you have the desire (or possibly the necessity) to continue this undertaking, here are some tips to help you along.

The more immersed you are in the language, the faster and easier you will learn. If you are living (even for a short time) in a German-speaking environment, you will have a leg up, but it takes a bit of discipline. As frustrating as it can be at times, try to only watch television and listen to the radio in German.

Concentrate at first on distinguishing sounds, then words. This is easier said than done! Even though the letters (or most of them, anyway) are the same as in English, they often somehow manage to sound different coming out of "foreign" mouths. Sounds are made in slightly different positions in the mouth, which, while they're basically the same sounds, they're not quite as easy to recognize. This will make it sound like the other person is speaking very quickly, but the truth is that you are simply listening slowly, due to the fact that you're having to match the sounds they're making with the sounds you're expecting, and when they don't match exactly it causes you to have to work harder.

Don't feel bad if you can't understand every word, or even if you miss words that you think you should have caught. When you're learning a language, you are listening to every sound, trying to separate out each word, and translate it. When you are fluent, you don't need to do that. You can "guess" at a word by only hearing a portion of it, so it isn't necessary to hear the whole word to understand it.

So since your listening skills are being strained, it's counterproductive (and extremely frustrating!) to try to catch every word. Instead, focus on picking out a word here and there. It doesn't matter if you can't follow every conversation. Learning to recognize individual words is a good way to speed up your listening skills and you'll find that it won't be too long before you graduate to being able to understand whole sentences.

If you don't live in a German-speaking place where it will be always in the background, you can still immerse yourself to a small degree. Find German videos online, German music or eBooks. It is much easier today than it ever has been before to find resources for spoken German, and the more you listen, even if you're not consciously learning, the faster you'll be able to pick it up in the long run.

Another way to improve your skills, specifically in vocabulary and sentence building, is to copy (preferably by physically writing them out) German stories or news articles (or lessons). Writing German sentences will give you a feel for the flow while teaching you word endings and vocabulary. Don't forget to stop and read the sentences out loud so you can practice your pronunciation at the same time! It's also important to get in the habit of analyzing sentences as you're reading or copying them. You don't want to do it necessarily with everything you read (or you'll quickly lose your desire to continue), but make sure you set aside some time to go through each word and select sentences to quiz yourself on what endings there are, what cases the words are in, why the word order is the way it is, etc. The more analytical you can be, the more it will make sense to you and the less "unnatural" it will feel to speak.

It probably won't feel like it's going as quickly as you'd like. Languages are incredibly complicated things with thousands of words to memorize, not to mention wrapping your mind around pronoun endings, tenses, and which prepositions go with which case. When speaking, if you're unsure of a word or a conjugation, it's better to toss in the English word than to halt the conversation while you look it up. Your listeners will probably either understand or be able to guess what you meant, and will most likely either provide the word for you or simply ignore the switch. The important thing is to be able to make yourself understood, not to be perfect. You forgive non-native English speakers when they make a mistake, so allow yourself some lapses as well. They are more likely to respect your commitment to learning than to deride your blunders.

You may feel like you're wasting your time and you'll never get there, but take heart. After all, if small children can learn German, surely you can too!

If you found this information helpful in any way, a review on Amazon is always appreciated!

www.ingramcontent.com/pod-product-compliance
Lightning Source LLC
Chambersburg PA
CBHW052204110526
44591CB00012B/2074